# Jazz Piano Comping for the Beginning Jazz Improvisor

For: Pianists, Vibraphonists, Singers,
Composers, Arrangers, and Wind Players

by Tom Anderson

ISBN 0-7935-5891-3

PUBLISHING, INC.

DISTRIBUTED BY

HAL•LEONARD™
CORPORATION
7777 W. BLUEMOUND RD. P.O. BOX 13819 MILWAUKEE, WI 53213

# TOM ANDERSON

TOM ANDERSON has a varied background in music which includes playing the piano, guitar, bass, and drums. He has earned degrees in Film and Television from Montana State University, Music Education from Minot State University, and the University of North Texas. Most recently, he completed a DMA in Choral Conducting from the University of Missouri-Kansas City.

He has taught at the junior high school and university levels and has introduced music to many people of all ages. Dr. Anderson has taught at the Penn State Schuylkill Campus and Eastern Washington University in Cheney, Washington. He lives in Spokane, Washington and keeps an active schedule as a performer. This includes playing guitar in the New Jazz Repertory Ensemble which is directed by Robert Curnow.

# FOREWORD

There are several sources available to a jazz pianist that are designed for the intermediate player. The most common format is a "voicings" book which suggests possible combinations of notes for chords. They are usually written for more advanced students. The authors of such books assume that the readers already understand basic chord construction, nomenclature, and harmonic function. But what does one do if he or she does not know this information? It is this author's desire to introduce jazz piano accompanying from the beginning or, as people in jazz might say, "from the top." If you do not know the difference between these chord symbols (or even know what a chord symbol is):

C   C7   Cmaj7   Cm7

then this book should be of help to you. The only knowledge necessary to begin studying this book is the ability to read music in treble and bass clef.

What is jazz piano "comping?" It is derived from the word "compliment." You are to provide a musical background that "fits" or is "correct." You are also to provide that background with a minimum amount of information - primarily chord symbols. If you are a pianist in a jazz ensemble or a jazz choir, you may have faced these letters with no idea as to what they represent. This book will give you some answers. Each section will build on the information which precedes it. Common jazz pieces are used as examples. You may have been or will be asked to play the accompaniment to one of these pieces. They have become classics or "standards" partly because of their interesting chords. Each example is notated with possible note choices for each chord and the melody. Have someone play the melody as you play the chords. You will be comping or complimenting them musically. Hopefully, this will be a beginning of a lifetime of musical activity. Let's begin...

# Table of Contents

ABOUT THE AUTHOR ................................................................. 2

FOREWORD .............................................................................. 2

CHAPTER 1: THE BEGINNING ................................................... 4

    COALITION OF COLORS (VERSION ONE) ......................... 10

CHAPTER 2: DOMINANT SEVENTH CHORDS ................................ 14

    PEANUT BUTTER BLUES ..................................................... 18

CHAPTER 3: MINOR SEVENTH CHORDS ................................... 20

    SPICE AND SPIRIT (VERSION ONE) ................................... 22

CHAPTER 4: MAJOR SEVENTH CHORDS .................................. 25

    SAD SATELLITE .................................................................. 28

CHAPTER 5: OTHER SEVENTH CHORDS ................................... 30

    FOND MEMORIES .............................................................. 35

CHAPTER 6: THE MUSIC OF DUKE ELLINGTON ...................... 38

    LEAVIN' ON A BUS ............................................................ 40

    COOL DUDE ...................................................................... 44

CHAPTER 7: NINTH CHORDS .................................................. 46

    HEAVENLY HANNAH .......................................................... 48

    CANDLELIGHT SERENADE ................................................. 54

CHAPTER 8: EXTENSIONS AND POLYCHORDS .......................... 56

    COALITION OF COLORS (VERSION TWO) ....................... 61

    SPICE AND SPIRIT (VERSION TWO) ................................. 65

CHORD SYMBOLS/ NOTES/ VOICINGS ..................................... 69

SONG EXAMPLES ON PLAY-A-LONG RECORDINGS ..................... 71

GLOSSARY ............................................................................... 71

# Chapter 1: The Beginning

Where does one begin when starting a new activity? Some of this information may be too basic for you so feel free to move into the new material once you understand a concept. Progress at your own rate and review as much as is necessary. Here are some general comments on jazz piano comping:

- you are expected to provide an accompaniment by interpreting chord symbols which are normally written above the music

- you are to improvise a rhythm so that it "fits"

- both hands are to be used when comping but you are not to double the bass part with your left hand

- use the sustain pedal sparingly unless you are playing a ballad

- generally, play in the middle area of the piano. Mainly an octave above or below Middle C

- listen, listen, listen to good jazz pianists who are an integral part of the rhythm section and accomplished "compers"

Here is some basic information that should be of help. Again, feel free to move ahead at your own rate. A CHORD is three or more notes played at the same time.

Figure 1

A disadvantage facing beginning jazz pianists is that most jazz chords are constructed with more than three notes. You can play jazz chords by using only three notes - which will be discussed later - and sound "authentic." However, you must know which three notes are appropriate. Have the patience to study the material to learn this information.

A CHORD SYMBOL is used to describe the construction of a chord.

C      E7+9   Go7

These are written above the melody. As a jazz pianist, you are expected to know what they represent.

In order to study the construction of chords, you should be familiar with the idea of an INTERVAL. An interval is the distance between two notes. A HALF-STEP is the smallest interval on the piano keyboard.

FIGURE 2

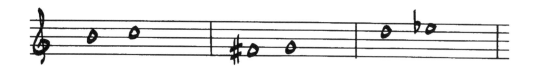

One method of analyzing chord construction is to count half steps between the notes of a chord. A chord that is made up of only three notes is called a TRIAD. While this type of chord is not widely used in jazz, you do need to be familiar with its formation before notes can be added to it or it can be varied as part of a more complex chord. One of the most common types of triads is a MAJOR CHORD.

FIGURE 3

The chord symbol for a major chord is a single letter. This letter represents the root note of the chord. Play the chord with your right hand and play the chord's root with your left in the lower section of the keyboard.

FIGURE 4

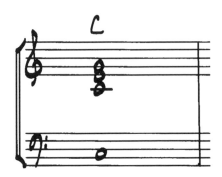

The third of a major chord is four half steps above the root. The fifth is three half steps above the third. Therefore, to construct a major chord, play the root (the same letter used in the chord symbol), count up four half steps to play the third, and three half steps above the third to play the fifth. Then play these three notes at the same time to play a major chord.

Here are the major chords based on the "white notes" of the piano. Play them with your right hand and double the root with your left in the lower portion of the piano.

FIGURE 5

While major chords are not widely used in jazz, they are very common in rock music. Here is the introduction to "Proud Mary" which uses major chords exclusively. Play the chords using the rhythm that is indicated.

EXERCISE 1

While this is not jazz piano comping, it is at least a step towards accomplishing that because you are interpreting chord symbols to determine what notes are to be played. Here are the major chords with roots that are "black notes" on the piano keyboard.

FIGURE 6

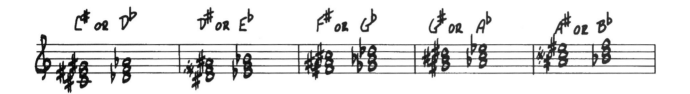

Again, using rock music as an example of music that uses major chords, play the following chord progressions. Can you think of rock songs that use these three chords that are played with this rhythm?

EXERCISE 2

Another common type of triad is a MINOR CHORD.

Figure 7

The chord symbol for a minor chord is a letter representing the root which is followed by: - (a dash), m, mi, or min.  Jazz pianists are faced with various chord symbols that indicate the same type of chord.  Jazz composers and arrangers use this system of short-hand but are not consistent when selecting chord symbols.  Be prepared for several possibilities for many types of chords.

The distance between the root and third in a minor chord is three half steps.  It is four half steps from the third to the fifth.

FIGURE 8

Here are the minor triads with roots that are "white notes" in the piano keyboard.

FIGURE 9

Play the following chord progression made up of minor chords.  Each slash represents one beat.

EXERCISE 3

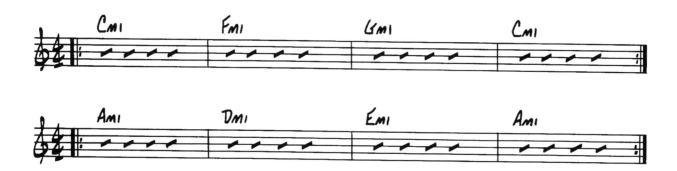

It is very important to know what notes make up each chord. You will be expected to quickly play the proper notes as indicated by the chord symbols. Make sure you know the roots, thirds, and fifths of all major and minor triads and can play them when looking at the corresponding chord symbols.

Here are the minor triads with roots that are "black notes." Play Exercise 4 after studying them.

FIGURE 10

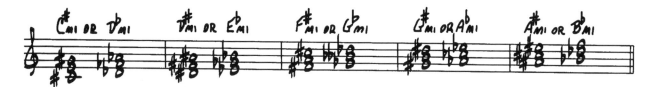

EXERCISE 4

Each of the examples of triads have been written in ROOT POSITION. The lowest note of each chord is the root. This does not always have to be the case and actually makes for awkward movement from one chord to the next (the movement being known as VOICE LEADING). However, you must know the notes in each major and minor triad before attempting to construct more complicated chords.

As written previously, most chords in jazz have more than three notes. This is one reason jazz harmony sounds so rich and full. The following arrangement of "Coalition of Colors" uses only major and minor chords in root position. While these chords are harmonically correct, this does not sound like "authentic" jazz. One of the last arrangements in this book is the same song with more advanced jazz harmonies. There will be a step-by-step procedure used to introduce these more advanced chords.

Play the chords which are notated below the melody. Notice the chord symbols and try to remember which notes are in each major and minor chord. Sing the melody or have someone play it as you play the chords. You are doing a very simple "comp" of this beginning level arrangement.

# COALITION OF COLORS (version one)

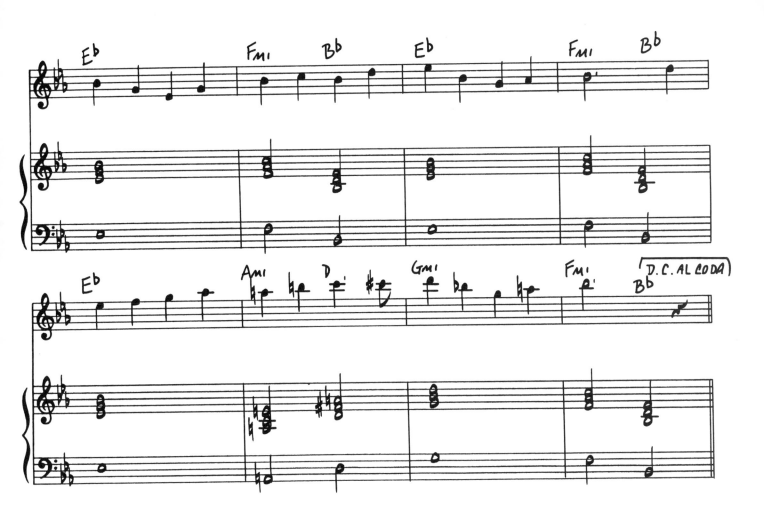

It sounds somewhat disjointed because you are moving quite far from chord to chord. That is a disadvantage when limited to playing chords in root position. Once you are familiar with the notes that make up the chord, you can put them in different order and still play the same chord. For example, here are two forms of a C major chord.

FIGURE 11

Here are two forms of an A minor chord.

FIGURE 12

When the third of a chord is the lowest note, the chord is in FIRST INVERSION. When the fifth is the lowest note, SECOND INVERSION is being used.

Play the following exercise and notice that root position, first inversion, and second inversion are included.

EXERCISE 5

Do you notice how much "smoother" it sounds when going from chord to chord when various inversions can be used? One element that helps to create this smoothness is to use COMMON TONES (or the same notes) between one chord and the next. For example, both C and F major chords contain the note C. That C remains in the same position when switching from the C to F major chords. Always look for common tones and try to keep them as a "pivot point" when moving from chord to chord.

Once you are familiar with the notes in each chord of "Coalition of Colors," play the accompaniment using various inversions for the smoothest voice leading possible. Look for common notes. For example, the first two chords, Eb and Cm, contain two common tones. Here would be one possible example of smooth voice leading where these two notes are in the same position in each chord.

FIGURE 13

What is the common tone from Cm to Gm? Can you think of an inversion to use for Gm that would have the note G as the highest tone? (first) Once you are familiar with inversions and common tones, your comping will have a much smoother sound.

# Chapter 2: Dominant Seventh Chords

As written previously, most chords used in jazz are constructed of more than three notes. A major or minor triad may be used as a first or last chord but are rarely included extensively. Therefore, to be a jazz piano comper, you need to be familiar with chords that have more notes than a triad.

If a chord symbol contains a letter (representing the root of the chord) followed by the number 7, it is describing a DOMINANT SEVENTH chord.

C7     F7     G7     A♭7

A dominant seventh chord in root position is made up of a major triad as the lowest three notes. The top note is a WHOLE STEP (two half steps) below the note an octave above the root.

FIGURE 14

In a dominant seventh chord, it is four half steps from the root to the third, three half steps from the third to the fifth, and three half steps from the fifth to the seventh. Dominant seventh chords are very common in jazz harmony as well as rock.

Here are the dominant seventh chords based on C, F, and G.

FIGURE 15

As you did with major and minor triads, familiarize yourself with each chord in root position before playing them in various inversions.

The roman numerals below each chord in Figure **16** represent the HARMONIC FUNCTION of each. In the key of C, the first note of the major scale (or I) is C, the fourth (IV) is F, and the fifth (V) is G. These notes correspond to the roots of the chords.

FIGURE 16

A jazz pianist needs to be familiar with this information because it helps for improvisation as well as determining which notes can be added to a chord.

A common chord progression in jazz and rock is the 12-BAR BLUES. The term "12 Bars" refers to a progression that is twelve measures in length. "Blues" is used because the original examples of this form were often slow, somber, and quite sad. Dominant seventh chords can be used exclusively when playing this chord progression.

Each of the following roman numerals represents one measure. Play the progression in the key of C using C7 for the I7, F7 for the IV7, and G7 for the V7.

EXERCISE 6

|     |     |     |     |
|-----|-----|-----|-----|
| I7  | I7  | I7  | I7  |
| IV7 | IV7 | I7  | I7  |
| V7  | IV7 | I7  | V7  |

There are several ways to play this progression. You could play four quarter notes per measure. You could play each chord on eighth notes which will produce progression used in many rock 'n' roll songs of the 1950's.

Try playing it in several keys. Use the first, fourth, and fifth notes of a major scale to determine the roots. For example, the I, IV, and V in the key of G would be G, C, and D. The I, IV, and V in F would be F, B♭, and C.

Inversions can be used with all form of chords when comping  As you did with major and minor triads, become familiar with the notes in the various dominant seventh chords and then arrange those notes so you are moving smoothly from chord to chord.  For example:

EXERCISE 7

Moving from one chord in root position to another in the same position rarely sounds "smooth."  Always look for common tones (the note C in C7 and F7) and the least amount of movement from one chord to the next (E to E♭ when moving from C7 to F7).

Here are four dominant seventh chords in various inversions so that the smoothest voice leading can be accomplished.

EXERCISE 8

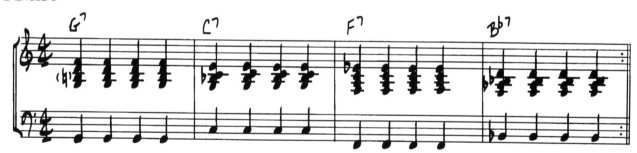

One rhythmic aspect of jazz that is predominantly used is SWING EIGHTH NOTES. When the word "Swing" is used to describe a piece of music, the composer or arranger is implying the following:

FIGURE 17

The eighth notes are <u>not</u> even.  The first is long while the second is short.  Listen to the music recorded by the Count Basie, Duke Ellington, and Woody Herman bands of the 1940's.  This treatment of eighth notes was very common.

When you "swing" the eighth notes, try not to analyze the feeling as much as emulate the rhythms used by the previously mentioned bands.  Look for the word "Swing" in the upper left hand corner of the music and adjust accordingly.

Swing eighth notes are used in "Peanut Butter Blues"  This is a tune very much like a typical Duke Ellington tune.  It is in the key of C and is a 12 bar blues.  You are to provide the happy rhythmic feel to make it sound like a "jam session."

Dominant seventh chords are used exclusively.  The I, IV, V progression in C is represented by the chords C7, F7, and G7.  The last two measures of the repeated section incorporates the chords C7, A7, D7, and G7 which are based on the first, sixth, second, and fifth notes of a C major scale, respectively.  These four chords make up a TURN-AROUND which is used to propel the chord progression back to the beginning I7 chord.

Play the chords only to "Peanut Butter Blues" as someone sings or plays the melody.

# PEANUT BUTTER BLUES

One question often asked by beginning jazz piano compers is, "What do I use for the rhythm of the chords?" This is probably the first time they are expected to not only determine the proper notes to be played but they must also improvise the rhythm. The melody of "Peanut Butter Blues" offers one possible solution: use it's rhythm as the rhythm of the chords. For example, the first four measures would be played as:

FIGURE 18

Continue using the melodic rhythm for determining when the chords are to be played. Complete the turnaround by playing the D7 and G7 on half notes. Is this beginning to sound like an example of "authentic" jazz piano comping?

Another possibility is to repeat a rhythmic motive and change the chords at the proper time. The rhythmic figure of a dotted quarter note followed by an eighth note could be used for the accompaniment of "Peanut Butter Blues."

FIGURE 19

The song examples in this book contain the melody and suggested voicings for each chord. Whole notes and half notes are used extensively to show the length of each chord. <u>You are not to use these long-valued notes as examples of "authentic" rhythmic jazz piano comping.</u> You are to provide the rhythmic interest by improvising an appropriate rhythm pattern that "sounds good."

That is what a jazz pianist does: plays the correct combination of notes for the proper length using an interesting rhythm. Again, listen to many examples of accomplished jazz pianists to gather ideas.

# Chapter 3: Minor Seventh Chords

Another four note chord commonly used in jazz is the MINOR SEVENTH chord. The chord symbol for this type of chord is a letter representing the root, followed by an "m," "min," or "-" which is followed by the number 7. Here are three chord symbols. Each represents a C minor seventh chord.

Cm7           Cmin7         C-7

The bottom three notes of a minor seventh chord in root position are the same as a minor triad. The top note is a whole step below the note an octave above the root.

FIGURE 20

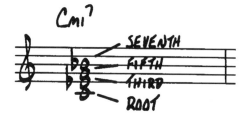

In a minor seventh chord it is three half steps from the root to the third, four half half steps from the third to the fifth, and three half steps from the fifth to the seventh.

As with all types of chords, become familiar with minor seventh chords in root position and then use inversions for smooth voice leading between different chords. Play the chords with your right hand and the roots with your left hand in the lower portion of the piano. Each slash represents a beat. Play the chords using a quarter note rhythm.

EXERCISE 9

Notice in the second version that common tones are used from chord to chord (F and D in Dm7 to Gm7) and the closest note is selected when a note has to change (Bb to Ab in Cm7 to Fm7). This practice helps to provide for the smoothest possible voice leading. Accomplished jazz piano compers are capable of doing this.

Another aspect of harmony that should be understood is the harmonic function of a chord. This was touched upon when the I, IV, and V chords were used for a 12 bar blues.

Each chord within a key serves a different function and can be described with a chord symbol or Roman numeral. In the study of traditional harmony, Roman numerals are frequently used to label chords. A main concern of someone analyzing a piece of classical music is the description of a chord within a key. Numbers in upper case (I, IV, V) indicate major chords while lower case numbers (ii, iii, iv) describe minor chords. A lower case number followed by a circle ( vii o) is a type of diminished chord which will be described later.

To construct the chords within a key, you evenly stack the notes from the scale on top of one another and use the notes of the scale for the root of each chord. Here are the chords in the key of C major with the corresponding chord symbols and Roman numerals used to describe their placement within the key. The I maj7 (Cmaj7) and IV maj7 (Fmaj7) chords will be described in the next chapter. The viiø7 (Bø7) will be introduced in a later chapter.

FIGURE 21

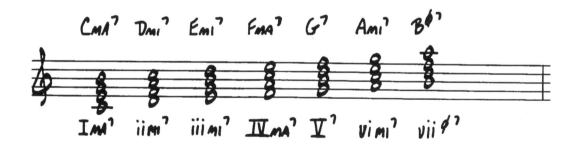

"Spice and Spirit" is a version of a song played  by many non-pianists because they find it easy to play by "ear." While one may have grown tired of hearing it, it can be used to illustrate a common chord progression with a sense of harmonic function (I, vi7, ii7, V7). Most people probably do not realize they are playing the first, sixth, second, and fifth chords in C major but, hopefully, you can see their placement within this key. Also, the chords sound good because smooth voice leading is being used.

# SPICE AND SPIRIT (version one)

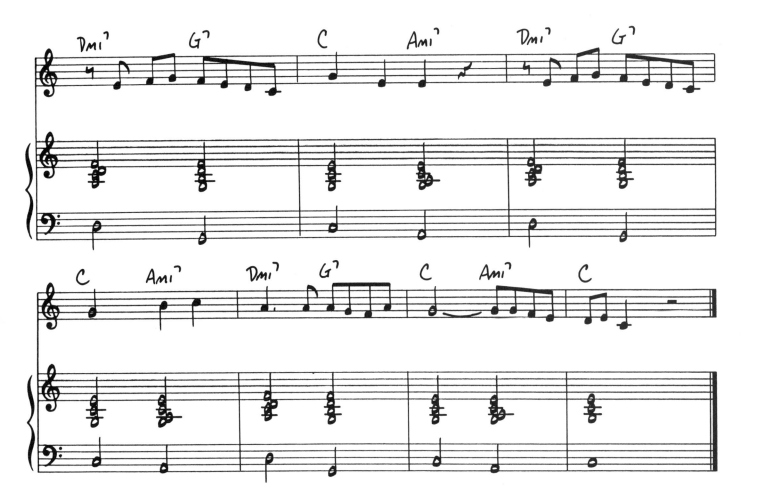

*Did you realize that this song is usually played with swing eighth notes?*

This song is used as the final example to this book to illustrate that even a simple song like "Spice and Spirit" can be made harmonically interesting by incorporating jazz chords. You might want to play that version at this time to see where you are heading. Each of the chords used in this final arrangement are described before they are included. They do help to brighten up this "tired, old song."

# Chapter 4: Major Seventh Chords

Another common four-note chord used in jazz and other forms of popular music is the MAJOR SEVENTH CHORD. It has a "pretty" quality although the outer two notes in root position have a clashing sound. By adding the middle two notes, the chord is now "mellow."

As with the minor seventh chord, the major seventh is represented by several chord symbols.

Cmaj7          CM7          CΔ7          CMa7

Each of these chord symbols represents the same combination of notes and, again, a jazz pianist is expected to be familiar with all of them. Here are the notes, in root position, of a C major seventh chord.

FIGURE 22

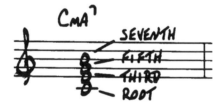

The bottom three notes are the same as the major triad. The top note is a half step below the note an octave higher than the root. It is four half steps from the root to the third, three half steps from the third to the fifth, and four half steps from the fifth to the seventh.

The chords Cmaj7 and Fmaj7 are the only major seventh chords using only "white notes."

FIGURE 23

All other major seventh chords include a sharp or flat to achieve the proper construction.

While it may be necessary to play major seventh chords initially in root position to become familiar with them, it is usually desirable to play the chord without the root in the right hand. The root is to be played with the left hand, or by the bassist. Try to avoid playing the root in the right hand.

EXERCISE 10

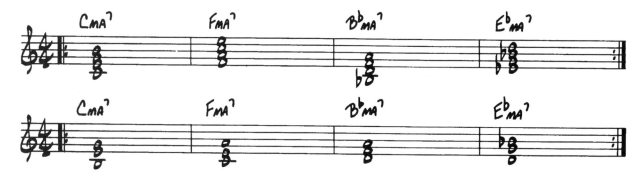

Notice how much smoother the second four measures sound as compared to the first. Common tones are used from chord to chord and the root is not part of the right hand voicing.

As previously mentioned, major and minor triads are rarely used in jazz harmony. It is common practice for jazz pianists to add notes when they encounter chord symbols such as:

C     F     Em     Am

The seventh of each chord is usually the first thing to be added to provide a fuller sound. Therefore, a jazz pianist would play a CΔ7, FΔ7, E-7, A-7 when seeing the previous chord symbols.

FIGURE 24

Notice that the roots are not included in these voicings but the sevenths have been added. Playing only major and minor triads does not have an "authentic" jazz sound.

Major seventh, minor seventh, and dominant seventh chords are all used in "Sad Satellite." Feel free to play each in root position before playing the suggested voicings. The root is often not part of the right hand voicing so you may be confused (at first) as to which notes are part of each chord.

This song is also a good example of the harmonic function of "Spice and Spirit" : IΔ7, vi-7, ii-7, V7. Also, the ii-7 to V7 chords in various keys are evident. A jazz musician must become familiar with a rapid succession of keys. As you will soon see, jazz harmony is usually very advanced - but worth studying!

Rhythmically, this song does not have to be much more complicated than the half notes and whole notes used for illustration. Again, a swing feel is to be incorporated for the eighth notes.

# SAD SATELLITE

29

# Chapter 5: Other Seventh Chords

It is important to understand the construction of seventh chords because they are so common in jazz. Dominant seventh, minor seventh, and major seventh chords are the most widely used. There are also variations of these types of chords.

When playing jazz or rock music, you will sometimes see a chord symbol that contains the letters "sus":

C7sus   C7sus4

This is a SUSPENDED CHORD. The note that is being suspended or raised is the third note of the scale.

Chords are usually constructed by "stacking" notes that are a third apart. This is called TERTIAN HARMONY which is based on the interval of the third. It has been used for several centuries of Western music. Dominant seventh, minor seventh, and major seventh chords in root position are examples of tertian harmony.

The suspended note is one half step above the major third of the chord. It is the fourth note of the major scale.

FIGURE 25

A common chord progression is to have the suspended fourth resolve to the third of the chord.

EXERCISE 11

It is important to think numerically when considering the placement of a note within a scale. These numbers are often included in jazz chord symbols.

FIGURE 26

Notes that are "above" the first octave can be used in jazz harmony so do not stop counting at "8" when thinking of the numbers of a scale. These notes can be played within an octave of the root but they are still classified as "9", "11", or "13". Actually, if you consider that 2=9, 4=11 and 6=13, you may have an easier time of working with these numbers when they appear in a chord symbol.

Composer and arrangers use both "♭" and "-" to represent a note that is lowered by one half step. The symbols "+" and "#" both indicate that a note is to be raised by a half step. Notice which note of the scale is to be altered and then determine if it is to be lowered or raised.

One chord that has an altered note is a HALF DIMINISHED chord which is also known as a MINOR SEVENTH, FLAT FIVE chord. Both of these chord symbols can represent this type of chord.

Aø7     Am7♭5

To form this chord, play a minor seventh chord and then lower the fifth by one half step.

FIGURE 27

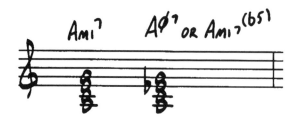

Again, it is extremely important for you to be familiar with which notes make up all dominant seventh, minor seventh and major seventh chords before altering them. You will soon see how chords with raised and lowered notes are common in jazz harmony. They are one of the aspects that adds interest to these chords.

A minor seventh, flat five chord will often be followed by a dominant seventh, flat nine chord.

FIGURE 28

The D7♭9 is actually a five-note chord but is played without the root in the right hand. Notice that the altered note (♭5) in the Am7♭5 (E♭) is also the altered note (♭9) in the D7♭9. That is one reason these two types of chords are used in succession. Another is that they serve as the second (iim 7♭5) and the fifth chords (V7♭9) of a harmonic minor key. The chords Am7♭5 and D7♭9 are the second and fifth chords of G minor, respectively.

FIGURE 29

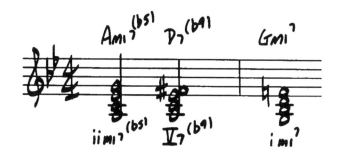

To determine the notes in a DOMINANT SEVENTH, FLAT FIVE chord, which uses the symbol G7♭5, first form a dominant seventh chord based on G.  Then lower the fifth by one half step.

FIGURE 30

You first need to know which notes make up a dominant seventh chord and then alter the appropriate note. All of the chords discussed in this chapter are used in "Fond Memories": 7sus, m7♭5, 7♭9 and 7♭5.  Each of them are based on various seventh chords.

The final chord of this arrangement does not include the seventh.  It is a SIXTH CHORD.  The only chord symbol representing this type of chord is formed by the letter of the root note followed by the number 6.

C6

This chord is formed by playing a major triad and adding the sixth note of a major scale.

FIGURE 31

Sixth chords can be played in place of a major seventh when encountering the chord symbol for a major chord.  Also, you can alternate between the seventh and sixth when comping major chords.

EXERCISE 12

A sixth chord, like a major seventh chord, has the sound of "finality".  They are often used as the last chord of a piece because of this characteristic.  Feel free to add this note to major chords if it "sounds right".

# FOND MEMORIES

# Chapter 6: The Music of Duke Ellington

While many composers, arrangers and band leaders have contributed to the evolution of jazz harmony, it would be difficult to name a more significant figure for this advancement than Duke Ellington. He served as each of the three functions and it can be argued that his contribution is significant for all 20th Century music.

Ellington's music serves as good examples of interesting jazz harmony. He was adventuresome in his combination of notes (harmony) and instruments that played those notes (arranging). Members of his band stayed for many years so he could tailor his compositions and arrangements to best fit their abilities. As with the study of all music, listen to examples of the highest quality. This is the case with the music of Duke Ellington.

The next tune, "Leavin on a Bus" is based on the same chord changes as are used in the famous tune named "Take The 'A' Train." While the song "Take the 'A' Train" was not written by Ellington, it was one of the most popular pieces played by his band. One element of this classic, that is evident in many songs of this era, is its form. If you were to label each eight-measure section with a letter (with A being the first), "Take the 'A' Train" has the form of AABA. The first eight measures is repeated and return at the end. The B section is called the BRIDGE. It is a contrasting section that helps to add variety to the song's form. You will often hear a musician discuss the bridge of a song - sometimes because it is difficult to play or remember.

The construction of each chord in "Take the 'A' Train" has been discussed in previous chapters. The sixth chord is used extensively which does have a "1940s" sound. The melody can be a good source for determining how a chord is to be altered. For example, the G# in the third measure is enharmonically the same pitch as the ♭5 in D7♭5 chord (A♭). The second to the last note of the bridge (A♭) is the ♭9 of a G7 chord. Feel free to add these notes to your chords.

Notice the chords used in the first ending: C6, A7, Dm7, and G7. This is a commonly used turnaround: I, V17, iim7, V7. It can sound stagnant to simply stay on the I chord at the end of the first A section. Also, there is nothing to "propel" the chords back to the beginning if a turnaround is not used.

Here is the same turnaround in various keys. Play through them by reading the chord symbols.

EXERCISE 13

|  | I | V17 | iim7 | V7 |
|---|---|---|---|---|
| F: | F6 | D7 | Gm7 | C7 |
| G: | Gmaj7 | E7 | Am7 | D7 |
| B♭: | B♭6 | G7 | Cm7 | F7 |
| E♭: | E♭maj7 | C7 | Fm7 | B♭7 |

While you are expected to improvise the rhythm when comping, you may be surprised by how simple and repetitive that rhythm can be and still keep the listener's interest. For example, try using the rhythm of:

when playing "Leavin' On A Bus". Change the chords at the appropriate time and don't be afraid to create syncopation. That is one of the joys of playing jazz - the driving and sometimes unexpected rhythm.

# LEAVIN' ON A BUS

41

The next song, "Cool Dude," is played to the same changes as are used in another famous song entitled "In a Mellow Tone." It is a good example of how music with relatively simple chords can become a jazz classic. Not all of Ellington's music used complex chords that were changed rapidly. And yet, a piece such as this can "stand the test of time" because it is interesting - to the listener and performer.

It can be surprising to learn that a jazz pianist can play a full sounding comp by using only two notes from the chord: the third and seventh. When you can correctly select these pitches, you are providing the most "significant" elements of the chord.

Play the following exercise with the suggested notes in the right hand and the root in the left. Only the thirds and sevenths are played but each chord sounds "complete" because everything that is necessary is played. Each slash represents a quarter note.

EXERCISE 14

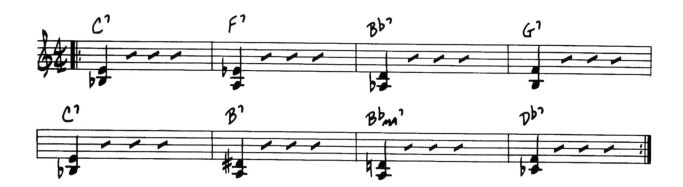

This two-note voicing is used for most of "Cool Dude." It is surprising to hear how only two notes can form a fairly complete sounding chord if only the third and seventh are used.

This comping rhythm is similar to one used by guitarist Freddie Green who played in the Count Basie band for over fifty years. He would play chords on quarter notes in the guitar's lower register which provided a constant, stable rhythmic pulse. It was very effective and an integral part of the Count Basie sound. Use detached quarter notes when playing the chords. The only new type of chord introduced in this song is in the sixth measure from the end. Its chord symbol is:

Do7

A circle followed by a 7 (with no line through the circle) is a FULLY DIMINISHED SEVENTH chord.  The only interval used to construct this chord is a minor third which is three half steps apart.

FIGURE 32

The difference between a half diminished and fully diminished seventh chord is the seventh.  In the first, it is a whole step below the note an octave above the root.  In a fully diminished chord, it is three half steps below that note.

FIGURE 33

The only chord symbol for a fully diminished seventh chord is a circle followed by the number 7.  Notice whether or not there is a line through the circle because that changes the quality of the chord.

# COOL DUDE

# Chapter 7: Ninth Chords

Jazz chords often include notes that are numerically higher than an octave. As had been previously mentioned:

9th = 2nd

11th = 4th

13th = 6th

These notes do not have to be over an octave above the root. Use your ear to help determine their placement. It sounds good to place the note within the other pitches of the chord.

FIGURE 34

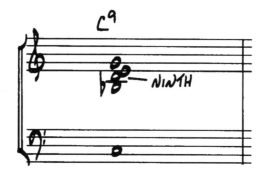

It usually does not sound good to have the ninth in the lower portion of the chord, next to the root.

FIGURE 35

Small intervals can sound "muddy" in the bass register.

The ninth used in the next tune, "Heavenly Hannah," is a flatted ninth on a dominant chord. Notice how this chord often is preceded by a minor seventh flat five chord. Again, it is the iim♭5 chord followed by the V7♭9 of a minor key. The second and fifth chords of G, C and B♭ minor are used in this song. The chords do not have to resolve to the im7 so be aware of each chord's harmonic function.

The only new type of chord introduced in "Heavenly Hannah" is a DOMINANT SEVENTH, SHARP FIVE chord. Here are three possible chord symbols that represent this type of chord are:

G7#5          G7+          G7aug

An augmented chord has the fifth raised by one half step.

FIGURE 36

"Heavenly Hannah" uses the same changes as the tune "Stella by Starlight," which is usually played as a ballad. As an alternative, after you have practiced it at a slower tempo, play it with a moderate swing beat. It "works" at that tempo as well. The chords should be played percussively with some syncopation at this faster tempo.

# HEAVENLY HANNAH

One important factor to consider when playing a ninth chord is the quality of the seventh. This note is sometimes a B and other times a Bb in the following chords:

Cmaj9  C9     C7b9  C7+9  Cm9

When "maj", "ma", "M", or a triangle appears in the chord symbol, the seventh is a major seventh.

FIGURE 37

When only numbers are used in a chord symbol, the seventh is a dominant seventh.

The ninth is a whole step above the root if the number 9 is used. It is lowered by one half step if a "b" or "-" precedes it. The ninth is raised by a half step if "#" or "+" appears before it.

FIGURE 38

The lower four notes of a MINOR NINTH chord in root position are the same as a minor seventh chord. The ninth is a whole step above the root.

FIGURE 39

As with seventh chords, all of the notes do not have to be present to create a full sound.  The third, seventh and ninth of the chord should be played to produce the proper quality.  Also, you do not have to always play the chord in root position.

While it is not the desire of this author to write yet another "voicings" book, there are some chords that sound "authentic" in one combination of notes.  That is true with a DOMINANT SEVENTH, SHARP NINE chord.  Your right hand should play the chord using these notes:

#9

♭7

3

A D7#9 would be played as:

FIGURE 40

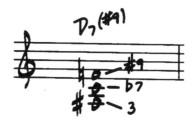

One way to think of the notes in this type of chord is that you play the major third on the bottom and the minor third on top.  There is a dissonance between these notes but that is what gives this chord some harmonic "bite".

EXERCISE 15

The previous exercise does not have smooth voice leading because of the large leaps from chord to chord.  But this voicing does sound "appropriate".  Notice how the interval of the fourth is an important factor for this chord's sound.

A practice used for writing chord symbols that is becoming more common is (for lack of a better term) the SLASH CHORD.  This type of symbol contains two sets of information with a diagonal line (or slash) in between.

C/D          Bm7/E          Cm7♭5/F          F/B♭

The material to the left of the line indicates the chord. The letter to the right is the bass note. Jazz arrangers and composers often use the sound of a bass note that is not the root of the chord.

The notes for the previous "slash" chord symbols would be:

FIGURE 41

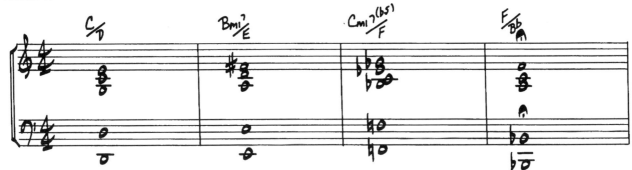

None of the bass notes are part of the chord. This is one of the reasons this type of chord sounds so interesting.

The eighth note feel for the next tune, "Candlelight Serenade" (played to the same changes as used in "The Shadow of Your Smile") is not swing. They are to be played evenly. If you were playing with a drummer, he or she would play even eighth notes on the hi hat or ride cymbal.

Try this simple comping rhythm when playing this song. Even repetition of the rhythm:

and changing the chords at the appropriate time would be effective. Remember, you are to compliment the person singing or playing the melody. If you would like, remove the tie and use this rhythm:

Even this minor of an adjustment helps to create variety.

There are two chord symbols with #11 in parentheses: F9 (#11) and E♭9 (#11) . You are not playing the augmented fourth in the suggested voicing. That note is contained in the melody. Always look at the melody to see if there are notes that extend above the given chord symbol. These extensions will be discussed in the next chapter.

# CANDLELIGHT SERENADE

# Chapter 8: Extensions and Polychords

One of the fascinating aspects of jazz piano comping is that you never "arrive". There is never a final resting point where you can think, "Now I am playing chords exactly as they should be played with the perfect rhythm." Musicians constantly learn and grow as players. That is one of the reasons music can be so satisfying (and at the same time frustrating) and truly a lifelong endeavor.

You have already studied the two pieces used for illustration in this chapter: "Coalition of Colors" and "Spice and Spirit". However, when they were first introduced, the chords were quite simple. That is not the case in this chapter. The chords used here have either been introduced, or will be, before you play the arrangements.

EXTENSIONS are used extensively in these two songs. These are chords that include notes above the root's octave. This would include NINTH, ELEVENTH and THIRTEENTH chords. Remember, a ninth is the same as a second, the eleventh is the fourth and the thirteenth is the same as the sixth. These notes do not have to be played in the octave which is over eight notes above the root. Like the dominant seventh and ninth chords, the thirteenth chord has only the number 13 following the root's letter for the chord symbol.

C13

When only the number is used, that designates that a dominant seventh is to be included (and not major seventh).

FIGURE 42

Like the seventh, ninth and eleventh chords, the thirteenth chord does not have to contain all the notes to sound complete. And like the dominant seventh, sharp nine chord, there is a voicing that is used almost exclusively when playing a thirteenth chord.

It is played as:

FIGURE 43

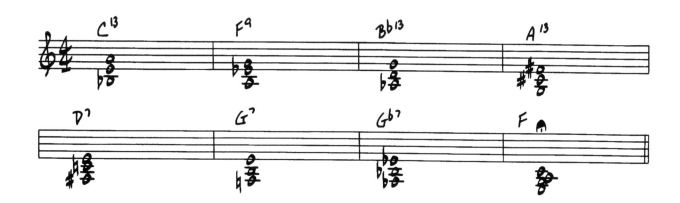

Again, notice how the interval of the fourth is used for this voicing. It helps to give the chord an "open" sound that has been more common in recent jazz history.

Feel free to play thirteenth chords even when a dominant seventh chord is suggested. The added notes such as a ninth or thirteenth will give your jazz piano comping a more "advanced" sound.

EXERCISE 16

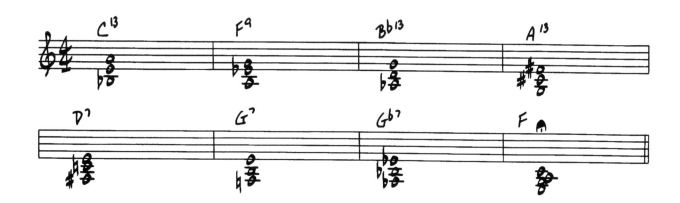

Do you know what notes of the chord have been added to the voicings in the second line? As a jazz piano comper, you are expected to add notes that sound "correct".

Another type of chord in this arrangement of "Coalition of Colors" is a SIX/NINE chord. It is formed by adding the sixth and ninth note of a major scale to a major triad. The chord symbol for this type of chord is a letter representing the major triad followed by the numbers 6 and 9.

FIGURE 44

This chord has a sound of "finality" and can be used as the last chord of a piece if it ends on a major chord. It also can be used to add interest to a sixth chord - such as the first chord of "Take the 'A' Train".

As a jazz pianist, you must be able to interpret how the extension notes are being altered. Again, a "+" or "#" is used to raise a note by a half step and "-" or "♭" means that the note is to be lowered by that interval. The last chord of the bridge in this arrangement has the following chord symbol:

$$B♭9♭13$$

First, look at the information that tells you how the basic chord is to be constructed and then play an appropriate voicing.

FIGURE 45

After that, think of a voicing that could be used without the altered extension.

FIGURE 46

Finally, alter the the extension as indicated by the chord symbol.

FIGURE 47

At this point, this appears to be a cumbersome process. Eventually, it should not take you too long to immediately interpret chord symbols - even with altered extensions. They are not widely used so you simply need to prepare for them as you are playing a piece for the first time.

The eleventh is often altered in jazz harmony. Many composers and arrangers incorporate the sound of the raised eleventh or SHARP ELEVENTH.

FIGURE 48

One of the reasons for this is that the fourth (or eleventh) note of the scale does not sound "good" when played in a chord or melody. It can be used as a passing note but does not lend itself as a "final resting place". By raising this note by a half step (#11), it dramatically changes the color of the chord or scale. Many jazz improvisers prefer using this note in their solos. Again, it provides a more "modern" sound.

For the study of extensions, you may want to view the chords as POLYCHORDS. This is where one chord is played on top of another. The chord symbol for a polychord looks like a "slash" chord. The difference is that the line is horizontal and not diagonal for a polychord's symbol.

$$\frac{D}{C7}$$

The left hand plays the chord below the line and the right plays the upper chord. After some study of extensions, you may be able to view a chord with a very complicated chord symbol such as:

$$C13\#11$$

as a polychord.

FIGURE 49

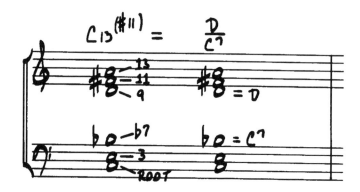

This type of chord is used on the last beat of the tenth measure from the end. It can be viewed as a relatively complicated chord or as a polychord.

$$A13\#11 = \frac{B}{A7}$$

The last two chords of "Coalition of Colors" can be separated as two chords. One is played by the left hand and one by the right. For the E69#11, the left hand is indicating an E major chord. The right hand is playing an F# major triad in second inversion. The same polychord is used for the final chord. It is a half step lower. Again, viewing relatively complicated chords as polychords may eventually save you time.

# COALITION OF COLORS (version two)

One of the first songs used in this book to illustrate chord functions was "Spice and Spirit."  Most beginning pianists learn the pattern of playing chords "on the white notes" and have a friend play the melody on that type of note.  With the proper knowledge and technique, this song can be used to show how jazz chords add interest to a song that may "get played too often".

Jazz chords can provide the proper dissonance or tension to interest the listener.  By adding the proper notes to a chord, the jazz pianist can play an accompaniment that truly compliments the performance.

Most of the chords in this arrangement of "Spice and Spirit" have been discussed.  Many of the more complicated chords can be viewed as polychords which will hopefully help you play them without too much difficulty. The second chord in the first measure is an example of a chord that looks complicated but can be played with four notes - if those notes are selected properly.  Remember, the third and seventh should be included most of the time.  Then it is a matter of interpreting the extensions and determine if they are altered by a "+",  #  , "-", or "♭".  Here the notes of the voicing are labelled.

FIGURE 50

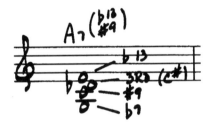

While D♭ is used for notational purposes, this note is enharmonically the same as C# which is the third of A7.

The second chord of the second measure has not been used before.  Again, first determine the notes played in the basic chord and then add the extensions.  A G13 would be played (from bottom to top) F, B, E because those notes correspond to the suggested voicing for a 13th chord: ♭7, 3, 13 (or sixth).  The only note that needs to be added to the G13♭9 is the ♭9 which is A♭.  This note appears in the middle of the voicing.  Remember, an extension does not have to be higher than an octave above the root.

FIGURE 51

The only other type of chord used in "Spice and Spirit" that has not been illustrated is the last chord in the eighth measure from the end.

$$G7\flat 9\flat 13$$

While this chord symbol looks complicated, when the notes are chosen one at a time, it is not difficult to select the proper pitches.

The basic chord is a G dominant seventh. The important pitches of the chord are the third (B) and seventh (F). The extensions are the flat nine (A♭) and the flat 13 (E♭). All of these "important" pitches are included in the suggested voicing.

FIGURE 52

This voicing is a good example of how extensions do not have to be played "in order", i.e. the eleventh must be higher than the ninth or the thirteenth must be above the eleventh, etc.

# SPICE AND SPIRIT (version two)

Now that you have been introduced to extensions and polychords, go back to some of the songs already presented and look at the extended notes as being part of two different chords or; polychords.

Using "Leavin' on a Bus" as an example, look at the second from the last note of the ninth measure from the end (G#). That is the $\flat$9 of a G7 chord. A possible chord that could be used for this note is:

G13$\flat$9

This chord adds pitches to the G7 chord and includes the melody note. It can also be viewed as a polychord.

FIGURE 53

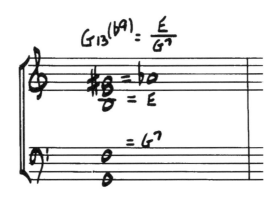

Try this voicing when you come to that note in "Leavin' on a Bus". It has a fuller, more "authentic" jazz sound than a G7 chord.

This procedure can be used in several songs already discussed. Look at the twelfth measure from the end of "Heavenly Hannah." The melody note is a D and the chord is A$\flat$7. The D is not part of an A$\flat$7 chord but is an extension of it: #11. Use this information to create an interesting jazz chord which can also be a polychord.

FIGURE 54

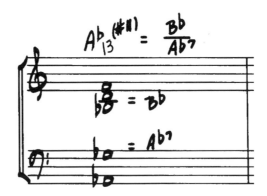

You do not have to include all the notes of each chord to form a polychord.  By playing the root and seventh of an A♭7 chord with your left hand (A♭ and G♭), you are implying an A♭7 chord.

There are two examples in "Candlelight Serenade" where polychords can be used. Again, look at the melody note to help determine the extensions.  A (#11) is written by the chord symbol in the sixth and fourth measures from the end to represent the melody note. Remember that a fourth is the same pitch as an eleventh.

$$+4 \; = \; \#11$$

Include this information in your chord symbol and voicing which creates a more interesting chord.

FIGURE 55

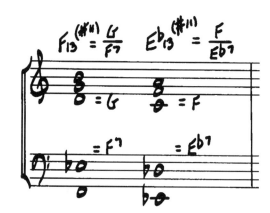

Try to include the extended notes of the chord if they are part of the melody.  Hopefully, by viewing these chords as polychords, you can play them quickly and use them as much as possible.

# Chord Symbols                 Notes                 Voicings

| Type of Chord | Chord Symbols |
|---|---|
| Major | C |
| Minor | Cm  C-  Cmin |
| Sixth | C6 |
| Dominant Seventh | C7 |
| Minor Seventh | Cm7  C-7  Cmin7 |
| Major Seventh | Cmaj7  C△7  CM7  CMa7 |
| Dom. 7th Suspended | C7sus  C7sus4 |
| Half Diminished | Cmin7♭5  Cm7♭5  Cø7  C-7♭5 |
| Diminished Seventh | Co7  Cdim7 |

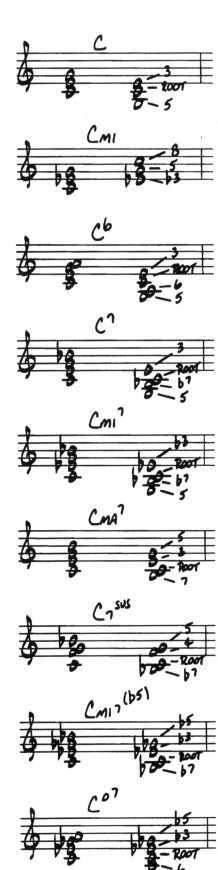

# Chord Symbols          Notes          Voicings

| Type of Chord | Chord Symbols |
|---|---|
| Dominant Seventh Aug. | C7#5  C7+  C7aug |
| Ninth | C9 |
| Major Ninth | Cmaj9  Cma9  C△9 |
| Minor Ninth | Cm9  Cmin9  C-9 |
| Dominant Seventh Flat 9 | C7♭9  C7-9 |
| Dominant Seventh Sharp 9 | C7#9  C7+9 |
| Dominant Ninth Sharp 11 | C9#11 |
| Thirteenth | C13 |
| Polychord | D̲ (C13#11)  C7 |

## Song Examples on Play-a-Long Recordings

There are many educational series of recordings produced that are of help to jazz musicians. Particularly for piano, one popular series is produced by Jamey Aebersold Jazz Aids. They are available from this address;

Jamey Aebersold
P. O. Box 1244
New Albany, IN 47151-1244

Each recording is a rhythm section (piano, bass and drums) playing chord progressions to songs or exercises. You are to provide the melody or improvisation in a "music minus one" setting. The recordings are produced in stereo with bass and drums on one channel and piano and drums on the other. In this way, if you want to practice comping with only bass and drums, you turn on that channel only. These recordings are excellent sources for hearing good jazz piano comping. They are worth ordering for this reason alone.

# Glossary

Bridge - musical material that follows the beginning section. Used for contrast.


Chord - three or more notes played at the same time.


Chord Symbol - letters and numbers used to describe the construction of a chord. Written above the music.


Comp - lit. "to compliment". Musically, it refers to providing a harmonic accompaniment.


Extensions - notes to be used in a chord that are numerically above an eight-note scale such as the 9th, 11th or 13th.


Harmonic Function - placement of a chord within a key.

Interval - distance from one pitch to another.  The HALF STEP is the smallest interval on the piano keyboard.  A WHOLE STEP is the combination of two half steps.

Inversion - a note of the chord other than the root is the lowest pitch.

Polychords - two chords played at the same time.  The chord symbol uses a horizontal line to separate the two chord forms.

Root Position - the lowest note of a chord is the root.

Slash Chord - a diagonal line is drawn through the middle of the chord symbol.  The information to the left of the line is the chord while the bass note is written to the right.

Swing Eighth Notes - eighth notes are not equal in length.  The first in the series of two is approximately twice as long as the second.  Rhythmically, swung eighth notes are:

Tertian Harmony - chords based on the interval of the third.  Major and minor triads in root position are examples of tertian harmony.

Triad - three-note chord.  MAJOR and MINOR triads are the most common in Western music harmony.

Turnaround - chord progression used at the end of a section to "propel" the music back to the beginning.  Used so a chord progression does not sound "stagnant".

12-Bar Blues - chord progression using I, IV and IV chords of a key.  Pattern is twelve measures in length.

Voicing - combination of notes played at the same time that specify a chord.